Help! I Have an
Attitude Problem

A Self-Help Book and Journal to Help
Teen Girls Overcome Negative Attitudes

Angela I. Gray MSW, EDS

ISBN: 9781082095924

<u>Dedication</u>

I am dedicating this book to all the young women who struggle with anger, resentment, and unforgiveness and have a negative attitude because of it. You are a beautiful person inside and out. Don't continue to let others win by holding on to your pain. It is your time to be healed.

Acknowledgement

Thank you to my mentor, soror, friend, and second mother, Dr. Venessa Brown for writing my foreword to this book. Thank you for always believing in me. Thank you to my supportive friends; Rosa Burton, LaDonna Whitner, and Ben Golley for reading my book and giving me honest feedback. I am so appreciative and grateful I have wonderful people like you in my life. Thank you to my supportive family. I love you so much Chris and Amoriah.

Foreword

Help! I have an Attitude Problem: A Self-Help book and journal to help Teen Girls to Overcome Negative Attitudes speaks to the commitment the author, Angela Gray has had from the moment I met her in the early 90's. It is with great respect and gratitude that I write this Forward for my student, mentee, soror, daughter and friend. Angela knows something about this topic. When I met Angela early in my college teaching career she was a student committed to finding her voice, winning and excellence. Her priorities were a little misplaced but her commitment to excellence and doing great things was not. She was a student that embraced my "directness" and instead of getting mad and having an attitude she trusted me to guide her to be the best social worker and advocate she could be. As I have followed her career her unwavering love for young people has been her guide to excel in education and social justice. Angela has been passionate and determined to equip herself with the knowledge, skills and abilities to lead students to success despite their life circumstances. I have been amazed at Angela's strength and her ability to actively listen to the verbal and non-verbal cries of our children. She has been innovative, creative, and driven to find ways to reach the youth most people would have given up on. As a person and professional she has lived by example. Her story of "checking your attitude" has been something she can write about because she has on occasions self-examined her own attitude and made a conscious decision to be someone to be sought out and selected to help youth. Angela has also been very honest with young people by sharing her own story with them and letting them know she too has had to "check her attitude". Angela's no-nonsense attitude has been the light that has guided so many youth through the dark tunnels of life. Her strategy is to teach youth to live in their own truths and to "check the attitude" so that others might see the true person they are. Many of our youth's life journey has been shaded by shame, hurt, violation and lack of love and their "attitude" is a shield to protect them from additional hurt.

To our Youth who read this, this self-help book and journal will be a great tool to assist you in your journey to finding your true self. The questions and reflection exercises will be opportunities for you to find your voice, cry if you need too, scream if you want, but more importantly, challenge yourself to face some of your fears, hurts and learn to forgive so that you can find that "attitude" that will unlock doors that welcome your gift to this life and allow you to walk in your purpose.

To the professionals who will be chosen to work with our amazing youth whose attitude is not allowing them to step into their greatness, this workbook will assist you in communicating, leading, and mentoring that special person who is hoping you don't give up on them. "Check that Attitude" and "Help I have an Attitude" are educational necessities for junior high and high school counselors, social workers, coaches, administrators, teachers and any personnel gifted the opportunity to work with our youth in finding their healthy attitude and voice to be change agents in the world.

Angela, thank you for your commitment to humanity and for being a light at the end of the tunnel for so many of our children. Your contributions to the literature and to everyday strategies for professionals are definitely needed as we learn new ways of communicating with our youth in this ever-changing world. Continue to write and encourage our youth to write so that their stories might be added lights to unknown darkness in this world.

Respectfully,

Dr. Venessa A. Brown
Associate Chancellor and Chief Diversity Officer
Professor, Social Work
Southern Illinois University Edwardsville
Edwardsville, Illinois

Table of Contents

Introduction

Have you ever been told, "You need to check your attitude, young lady!"? Well, this book is for you. You have been criticized multiple times about your negative attitude by teachers, family, and even friends. You lie to yourself and say, "I don't have an attitude problem. They have the attitude problem, not me." You are very defensive. When anyone tries to tell you about your attitude, you lash out at them. You often blame the other person, so you don't take responsibility for your actions. Sometimes you even isolate yourself from people to avoid what they have to say.

You might be thinking, "How do you know?" Well, I know because I used to be just like you. After some intense self-reflection, prayer, and counseling, my attitude has greatly improved. Now, I only get an attitude with someone when I feel they are being disrespectful to me. Even in those times, I try to take the high road because I refuse to let another person's negative energy get to me.

In this self-help book, I am going to have a heart to heart with you. We will talk about things that you may not want to discuss because they may be painful. You must get them out of you so your attitude does not continue to affect you in negative ways. You are going to have homework. I know you don't like homework, but I promise my homework assignments will be fun. To complete the homework, you will need a journal or notebook. They sell them very cheap at Dollar Tree or Walmart. You may also want to have some tissues handy.

Your Attitude Determines Your Aptitude

Have you ever heard the saying, "your attitude determines your aptitude in life"? What this means is that your attitude can determine how far you get in life. With your bad attitude, do you think you are going to be nominated for Homecoming Queen or Prom Queen? The answer is NO! Your peers won't want to nominate you because your attitude is horrible. They don't want you representing their class. Do you think you would get promoted as a manager or supervisor? The answer is NO! The company does not want someone with a negative attitude representing their company. They will lose customers because customers won't want to deal with your negative attitude. They will probably go elsewhere. My husband and I have high standards when it comes to customer service. We like to tip well if the customer service is above average, but if the worker has a negative attitude, we leave. We don't want to deal with someone who has a funky attitude after working hard all week. We work hard for our money so we don't have to put up with negative attitudes and neither will other customers put up with you.

My attitude prevented me from opportunities too. I remember when I was working at this agency. I snapped at my supervisor because I didn't like how he spoke to me. Now, looking back, he wasn't talking to me mean but because I was so defensive, I perceived he was being mean. I tried to get a job there after I graduated from college and was not hired. Mmmm, I wonder why I believe it was because of my negative attitude. I could have handled it differently. I could have talked to my supervisor with more respect. I apologized to him, but the damage was already done.

So, your anger can affect your aptitude. I see my students ruin opportunities because of their defensive attitudes. For instance, one of my students had an opportunity to go out of town for a school group she was involved in. She was smart and well-liked by teachers, but her negative attitude got in the way. The sponsor decided not to bring her in fear that she would act out on the field trip. The young lady was devastated. So, pay attention to how your attitude can affect your aptitude. You are the only person who can control how far you want to go in life.

Reflection

Think about a time when you were fired or not nominated for a position because of your attitude at school.

How did it make you feel?

_____

_____

_____

Homework

List any 5 ways regarding your attitude that can impact your personal life now and in the future.

_____

_____

_____

Anger Affects Your Attitude

Why are you so angry? Did someone leave you, offend you, or lie to you? We will discuss this more in the reflection/homework section.

Well! For me, I was angry and bitter because my father wasn't in my life growing up, I grew up very poor, and my mother had to do it all. It wasn't fair for her at all. I was mad as heck about it. My mother worked two, sometimes three, jobs at a time to provide for my sister and me. As a result, she didn't have a lot of time to spend with us because she had to work. I understood this as an adult, but it was difficult to understand it as a teenager. I spent a lot of time alone. My sister is seven years older, so I was too young to hang with her. Sure, I had friends and an older cousin, Fayshelle, or affectionately, "Tookie" to family, who I played with all the time. However, after she went home, I spent a lot of time alone. Maybe that is why I am a loner to this day. It is not a bad thing, but sometimes other people have a problem with it. Well, I don't. It keeps me out of mess and confusion. Are you a loner?

I didn't have much of a relationship with my father. I talked to him sometimes. I didn't see him from the age of 5 to 17 years old. He missed so many milestones in my life, such as the *First Day of Kindergarten*, *First Heartbreak*, *Prom*, *High School Graduation*, and *College Graduation*. It hurt. It hurt a lot. I tried to act like it didn't, but it did. The more I denied the hurt, the angrier I became over the years. Those are life events that I can't take back. My father made a lot of empty promises, such as sending me money, visiting me, or me visiting him. My father sent money, but it was not consistent. I didn't understand why he didn't visit me. He was only five hours away. If he didn't want to drive, he could have taken the train. The anger became more intense as I became a young adult.

In addition, anger can also be displayed in defensive attitudes. I wasn't the type of person to go off all the time. On the outside, I was nice and quiet, but on the inside, I was boiling with anger. The anger that I carried with me manifested as a defensive attitude. I expected the worse from others. Have you ever felt this way? Have you ever been asked, "Why are you so defensive?" This was me about twenty years ago. I had a chip on my shoulder. I used this defensive attitude to keep people from hurting me. I didn't want to be this way, but it was easier for me to control how others treat me. Do you do this?

<u>Reflection</u>

Think of someone who made you upset. How did it make you feel?

_____

_____

_____

_____

_____

Think of a time when you felt rejected or hurt. How did you deal with the pain?

_____

_____

_____

_____

_____

Homework

Write a letter to the person or people who hurt you or rejected you in your journal. Don't send it to them. The purpose of this is to process what happened to you.

_____

_____

_____

_____

_____

_____

_____

_____

_____

_____

_____

_____

Know Your Anger Triggers and Anger Cues

As humans, it is natural for us to become angry. We all get angry at some point. It is how we carry the anger that gets us in trouble.

When we say or do things when we get angry, we cannot take the words back. For example, expressing yourself on social media when you are angry can get you into a lot of trouble. I see it happen with my students all the time. They are angry at someone for something they said. Instead of talking it out in a calm fashion, they go on Facebook and slander the person. Then, they go back and forth with each other, repeating name calling and threats. Moreover, the threats become fights. Now, they fight at school and risk being suspended or expelled. All this drama could have been solved by talking it out with a mediator, such as a school social worker or counselor to resolve the issue.

There are signs that we get to let us know we are becoming angry. They are called anger cues. When you feel yourself getting angry, your anger cues serve as a warning to help you before you react to the anger. The cues could be the following:

- Red face
- Clenched fist
- Hands get red
- Lighting of face
- Eyebrows raised
- Fists are balled
- Heart racing
- Popping knuckles

Anger triggers are the same and they happen in order to let you know you are upset or irritated by something. It is good that you know what your anger triggers are in advance so you can be better prepared to respond. Anger triggers could be the following:

- When someone lies to you
- Your friends talk about you behind your back
- Someone puts something on social media about you that isn't true
- When someone steals from you

Reflection

What are your anger cues?

_____

_____

_____

What are your anger triggers?

_____

_____

_____

Homework

Write down how you would respond to anger triggers without becoming upset.

_____

_____

_____

_____

The Root of Rejection

Rejection is very painful. If you have never been rejected by someone, then you have no idea what I'm talking about. When you are rejected, it feels like someone took your heart out from your chest and stomped on it. I pray that you never experience pain like that because it could have long-lasting effects on you.

As I stated earlier, I experienced rejection through the absence of my father. I internalized the rejection I experienced and blamed myself. As a result, I isolated myself from others. I became very bitter. I didn't show it on the outside, but nonverbally. I used to roll my eyes, pout, and move my head around like I had something on my neck. As I look back on it, I really overreacted. My behavior was so silly. I didn't know how to carry my anger back then and I didn't talk about my feelings or emotions with anyone. I just kept it to myself.

I found it very difficult to trust others. I had low expectations that people would be there for me. I had my defenses up and I was not going to allow anyone to hurt me as my father did. I just counted on myself and didn't expect anything from anyone so I wouldn't be rejected. The rejection was too painful to endure. Instead of experiencing rejection, I didn't allow myself to ask anyone for anything. If I didn't have anything, then I would go without. I could have been starving and I would not ask anyone for help. I thought I was protecting myself from being hurt, but I was imprisoning myself. I didn't allow myself to feel, so I became numb on the inside. I expected to be let down. Even to this day, I have a difficult time inviting my family and friends to support me at events because of rejection. I don't want to hear all the excuses that people give when they can't attend your events, so I just don't invite them. Some people truly have good reasons as to why they can't attend or support, but others don't. They make up excuses instead of keeping it real and saying they don't want to attend. You know, I think people just want to be included or invited to something and they know full well that they don't want to go and support. I don't understand it and I never will. Do you have people in your life like this? If you do, just invite them to your events. If they come, then they come. If they don't, then they don't. At the end of the day, you have yourself. There may be times when you have to walk alone. It's ok. You are your own best friend. If you're not, you need to become it. Self-love is so important. If you don't have self-love, you can't love anyone else properly. Along with the lack of self-love, anger and rejection will plague your life if you let them.

<u>Reflection</u>

Have you ever been rejected?

_____

_____

_____

If so, by who?

_____

_____

_____

How did you feel about being rejected?

_____

_____

_____

_____

_____

<u>Homework</u>

Write a letter to the person or people who rejected you. Don't give it to them, but leave it in your journal.

_____

_____

_____

_____

_____

_____

_____

_____

_____

_____

_____

_____

A Negative Attitude Can Destroy Relationships

Do you push people away who love you or try to help you? People are put in our lives for a season, a reason, or a lifetime. Please remember this word of advice. The same friends you had in high school you may never speak to or see each other again. There are people in your life to help you, but you keep pushing them away. Don't do this. For example, you may feel like your Mom is nagging you about your attitude, but she is not. She is trying to help you. Please listen to her and anyone else trying to talk to you about your negative attitude. They have words of wisdom for you. They have been where you have been. Maybe it's a teacher, a school social worker, or counselor who is trying to help you.

Here are a few examples to show you how you push others away: The social worker or counselor calls for you or sends a pass to your class, you ignore them, and don't go. You avoid your teacher when he or she tries to talk to you. If they didn't care, they wouldn't try to help you. Please listen to them and talk to them. They love and care about you. Don't let your negative attitude destroy your relationships.

What about personal relationships? Have you ever had a guy not date you because of your attitude? Guys don't want to be bothered with your negative attitude. They want to have fun, not argue with you. They will probably tell you, "You're doing too much". This means stop giving them attitude. You may think it's cute but it's not. It makes you look like a fool. Guys will tell their friends that you were a headache, drama queen, or a nag. You don't want those labels, do you?

<u>Reflection</u>

Who have you pushed away?

_____

_____

What happened?

_____

_____

Have you ever been dumped by a guy for "doing too much"?

_____

_____

How did it feel?

_____

_____

<u>Homework</u>

Write a letter to someone who tried to help you. Tell them that you appreciate them, thank them, and ask for forgiveness.

_____

_____

_____

_____

_____

_____

_____

_____

_____

_____

_____

_____

Confess It!

So, we have discussed how rejection, anger, and a negative attitude can affect your aptitude in life. We also discussed anger cues and triggers. Now we are going to discuss how to overcome your negative attitude.

First, you must admit to yourself that you have an attitude problem. If you don't, you are in denial and can't be set free. You will continue to blame others for the actions that you created. It's time to take responsibility for your actions. I know you were hurt by others sbut holding on to the pain won't help you. People who have hurt you have gone on with their lives and they are not thinking about you. By holding on to the pain, you are giving all your power to your offenders who care less about you.

Hence, it is time to keep it real and let it out. You are doing this to heal you, not anyone else. This journey of healing is all about you. You may start feeling compassion for your offenders. For your accusers to hurt you, they must be missing something in their lives. There is a saying, "Hurt people hurt other people".

<u>Reflection</u>

Imagine being set free from all the hurt and anger in your life. Use three words to describe how you would feel.

_____

_____

_____

<u>Homework</u>

Say this out loud to yourself or confess it to someone who you can trust,

"I HAVE AN ATTITUDE PROBLEM!" Look in the mirror and say it as many times as it takes for you to believe it.

Power of Forgiveness

After you confess your problem. Let go and forgive. Forgiveness will set you free! You can't grow if you are holding unforgiveness in your heart. This includes forgiving yourself. Sometimes, we beat ourselves up internally by punishing ourselves for past mistakes. I used to do this a lot. I would forgive others but would continue to punish myself. Once I forgave myself, I felt so free. I let go of all the negative energy I was holding in my heart.

I forgave my father for not being in my life, but I will never forget how his absence made me feel. When I got older, I learned that my father had unresolved issues he was still dealing with. This does not excuse his behavior, however, it does shed light on his behavior.

I thank God I had a strong mother who didn't allow me to wallow in my pain. She was both my mother and father at the same time. My uncle, Bo, was also there to help me with performing fatherly duties. Through counseling, prayer, and writing in my journal, I finally forgave my father. Actually, the anger I had for him turned into compassion and sympathy. I felt sorry for him. So, forgive and move on!

<u>Reflection</u>

Imagine talking to your offenders about how they hurt you. What would you say and how would you say it?

_____

_____

_____

<u>Homework</u>

Say out loud in front of a mirror,

I forgive _____

for _____.

I forgive myself for

_____.

Find A Good Therapist

Therapy is good for the soul. I encourage you to find a good therapist you can talk to on a weekly basis. Ask your parents, school social worker, or guidance counselor to help you in locating a good therapist near you. There are several community agencies who take state Medicaid and private insurance.

There is nothing wrong with going to therapy. Make sure that you feel comfortable with your therapist. If you would prefer a female therapist, request one. Make sure your therapist listens to you and doesn't do all the talking. If you don't like your therapist, talk to him or her first before getting a new one. Talk to your therapist about how you feel if you don't like something that he or she is doing.

It is important to keep all your appointments and arrive on time. If you are running late, call him or her to let them know. Don't be more than 10 minutes late because they may reschedule your appointment.

<u>Reflection</u>

Think about any fears or hesitations you have about seeing a therapist. Write them down.

_____

_____

_____

<u>Homework</u>

- Google 3 therapists in your area and contact them.

- Ask the type of insurance they take.

- Make an appointment.

<u>Your Journal Is Your Best Friend</u>

My last strategy is journal writing. I believe that everyone should write in a journal. Journal writing is very therapeutic. It helps you to manage your feelings. It helps to release emotions that you have stored and is a good way to keep things private that you don't want to share with anyone. I suggest you hide your journal so no one can find it. Your journal is for your eyes only. Here are more benefits to journaling:

- Calms and clears your mind
- Releases pent up feelings and everyday stress
- Releases negative thoughts
- Explores your experiences with anxiety

(C. Ackerman, Positive Psychology program)

I started journaling when I was in college. I was going through some serious situations and I didn't want to talk to anyone about them. My journal literally became my best friend. I was able to write out my thoughts and feelings without getting criticized by anyone.

Journaling is very easy and relaxing. I suggest getting a journal with a lock. Just imagine you are talking to your best friend. I usually put the date at the top of the page, but you don't have to. You can journal at any time of the day or night. You don't need to use correct grammar, just write. Write about what upset you that day or write about anything. Afterward, you will feel so good venting about your day or situation. If you have friends who are struggling with their emotions, encourage them to journal also. They will be glad that you encouraged them.

Reflection

After you have journaled 3 or more times, what did you like about it? What didn't you like about it?

_____

_____

_____

_____

Homework

Go to your local Dollar Store and purchase a journal for $1.00. If you can afford it, purchase a journal from Walmart or Target.

Write 5 things you are grateful for in your journal.

_____

_____

_____

_____

_____

<u>Conclusion</u>

I hope you have enjoyed this self-help book and journal. Your healing is a process. It may take weeks, months, or even years. You are in control because your healing process depends on your willingness and readiness to be set free.

Moreover, you have your whole life ahead of you. Don't do anything to jeopardize your future. You are going to do great things. You are determined for greatness. Don't allow anyone to steal your joy. When someone steals your joy, then that person can steal your life.

Okay, now it is your turn to pass the torch to help other girls. Please purchase a book for someone to help them on their quest for healing. I hope you continue to write in your journal whenever you need to escape the pressures in your life. Don't forget to find a very good therapist who will be there to listen to you and help you. Talk to trusted adults who will hold you accountable. Remember, you are the pilot in your life as you are in control. Thank you for taking the time to read my book. I wish you all the best.

I AM EMPOWERED 2B ME

I DON'T CARE WHAT OTHERS

THINK, FEEL, OR SAY

ABOUT ME

I AM EMPOWERED 2B ME

Please contact Angela I. Gray
by email at:

empowered2beme@gmail.com

34

Made in the USA
Las Vegas, NV
30 November 2024

13009300R00028